Next-Level Income

How to Make, Keep, and Grow Your Money Using the 'Holy Grail of Real Estate' to Achieve Financial Independence

Christopher A. Larsen, M.B.A.

Dedication

In memory of my mother, Diane Larsen Gransky, who provided me with life as well as the foundation to get to where I am today; Christopher Strader, whose death inspired me to get the most out of life; and Lauren B. Larsen, my father, whose name I carry and hope to make proud.

Here's What's Inside...

About the Author

Christopher A. Larsen
Multifamily Real Estate Investor

Chris has been investing in and managing real estate since he was 21 years old when he purchased his first single-family rental property while in college. His family worked in and owned real estate, which gave him lessons at an early age on the value of having real estate as part of his portfolio. He honed his strategies through an MBA in Finance while at Virginia Tech, as well as over 20 years of, investing in managing and owning many different types of real estate.

Since 2012, Chris has focused exclusively on commercial real estate, specifically multifamily, which has included properties in North Carolina, South Carolina, Georgia, Texas, and Kentucky. In addition to management, he sat on the board of one of the largest mixed-use properties in downtown Asheville, North Carolina, and has developed single-family residential properties in partnership with his wife Jessica, who is an architect.

Chris has a B.S. in Biomechanical Engineering in addition to his MBA. After more than 15 years in the medical device field, he loves helping to educate others on how to achieve financial independence. Chris lives in Asheville, North Carolina with his wife and their two boys. He enjoys the outdoors, cooking, and spending time with his young family.

Acknowledgments

Thank you to Martin Gransky, my stepfather, who showed me the value of a strong work ethic and supported me during some of the worst times of my life. To Clint Provenza, who introduced me to racing bicycles and compound interest — these two things had a profound impact on my adult life. To Jessica Larsen, my wife, who is there on the good days and the bad days; she keeps me on the right track, as well as being an amazing and inspiring mother to our two active boys! You are awesome! To Caleb Welborn, marketing wizard and good friend, who was the inspiration behind this book and ultimately brought it to fruition.

Introduction

This book is not only about real estate. It is about the search for financial freedom and the freedom that it can provide in your life. I will share some of my life experiences and why I now invest in real estate, but I will also share why my mission is to help others achieve financial independence.

I've spent more than 15 years in the medical device industry working with doctors and surgeons. Most of these professionals not only went to grade school and college, but they also completed medical school, residencies and fellowships. Many did not complete this process and training until they were 35 years old. I have tremendous respect for our doctors in this country. (Don't ask me for medical advice; I didn't go to medical school.) I decided to devote my training over the last 20 years to becoming an investor. If you've read Malcolm Gladwell's book *Outliers*, then you've heard of the 10,000-hour rule. I've logged my 10,000 hours as an investor in the stock market, bonds, alternatives, and real estate.

In the following pages I will share my experiences of how I achieved financial freedom with you. I want to help you create a life of financial freedom so that you can live life on your own terms, and focus on your passions in life.

Chapter 1

How I Chose to Become an Investor

When we grow up, most of us are taught using the following sequencing: "Go to school, get good grades, go to college, and get a good job." Like a lot of eventual high-income earners, grade school was easy for me; I got good grades, tested well, was particularly good at math, and loved science. My family would say, "You'll be an engineer like your grandfather!" My grandfather was laid off and retired early at age 55, not because he wasn't good at what he did, but because he didn't want to play politics at work. Seeing this shaped my thinking from an early age as I realized that a high-income "secure" job doesn't guarantee wealth building, financial independence, or the freedom to live on your own terms.

I grew up in a firmly middle-class neighbor just south of Baltimore, Maryland, where my great-grandparents had a vegetable farm. My father was from a family of dairy farmers in Wisconsin; he was a salesman and entrepreneur who loved to enjoy life. Unfortunately, I never got to know him. Just after I turned age 5, he tragically died when the engine of his plane failed over Lake Michigan during a trip to visit his parents.

The family went on Social Security; we ate food out of cans, my grandmother made my clothes, and my mother stepped into the role of sole caregiver. Ultimately she married my stepfather, who became a father figure in my life as we got back on our feet. He was a contractor who built houses and specialized in remodeling high-end homes around Annapolis, Maryland at a late point in his career.

During the late '80s and early '90s, real estate was booming thanks to the baby boomers and their household-forming years. They were buying homes at a record pace. Builders and banks could hardly keep up. Remember Jimmy Dean sausage? Jimmy Dean had a construction company called J.D. Construction that was building neighborhoods near our hometown at that time. Both my parents went to work for J.D. Construction.

Things seemed pretty great until the Savings and Loan Crisis. The housing market dried up and they both lost their jobs as the company downsized.

From an early age, I realized that a high-income "secure" job alone doesn't guarantee wealth building, financial independence, or the freedom to live on your own terms.

Watching this process left an impact on me as I look back. I knew I didn't want to be in a position to lose my job. I also started to see the cycles in real estate and watched these unfold repeatedly over the following 20 years.

Whether it was genetic or due to my environment, I started my entrepreneurial streak at an early age. I never got a minimum-wage job like my friends. Instead I rented out my video games, had a paper route, and did landscaping on the weekends in the local upscale communities where my stepfather would often do jobs. Once I started racing my bike as a freshman in high school, I began to spend my afternoons training and weekends racing; on some weekends, I'd make as much as $500 in prize money. I learned that there were better ways to make money than working a nine-to-five job.

After grade school, I entered the Biomechanical Engineering program at Virginia Tech. In the first weekend before school, I joined the Virginia Tech cycling team. All I wanted to do at that point was race my bike. Life was great in college: studying, training, and racing. Then disaster struck when my best friend and training partner, Chris Strader, died of a brain hemorrhage in the summer between my freshman and sophomore years.

I lost my best friend, roommate, and training partner. I vowed to never let an opportunity pass me by again. Now I felt like I owed it to the world to live two full lives.

At this point, I knew that I didn't want to be an engineer and I decided that there was more to life than racing bicycles. I wanted and needed freedom to live life on my own terms. I loved the freedom of racing my bike and knew that I couldn't be an engineer working in a cubicle. A good family friend, the same one who had introduced me to cycling, gave me a Money magazine that illustrated the power of compound interest. I'll never forget the "aha moment" that inspired me. I opened a brokerage account, and in the fall of 1998, I began day trading and turned $20,000 into about $60,000. In addition to the day trading forums, my favorite websites were The Motley Fool and **www.retireearlyhomepage.com**, which was started by an engineer. I made a plan to become financially independent by 40 years old.

Financially independent people have assets that generate income, with a value that is at least equal to their expenses.

I also continued my entrepreneurial streak. I had a business selling loft beds to students at the beginning of each school year. In December 1999, I bought my first investment property, a three-bedroom townhouse where I rented out two of the rooms to friends.

Once I became a graduate student, I worked for the university. I remember the feeling of abundance from getting a $1,500 monthly paycheck to supplement my rental income and profits from my small loft business. My expenses were below my income. I figured that if I could maintain this type of discipline, I would always have money to invest.

It was during this time when I decided that I wanted to be an investor. I read over 250 books, went to seminars, and spoke to real estate professionals. I met Ray Alcorn, the man who "wrote the book on commercial real estate"; he suggested that I learn about property management to understand how to improve and optimize a property's income. Once I decided to become an investor, I read the *Rich Dad, Poor Dad* series and realized that I needed to become accredited.

An accredited investor has access to investments to which the average person does not. To become an accredited investor, a person must demonstrate an annual income of $200,000 or $300,000 for joint income over the previous two years, with expectation of earning the same or higher income. A person is also considered an accredited investor if they have a net worth exceeding $1 million, either individually or jointly with their spouse.

An accredited investor has access to investments to which the average person does not.

I knew that I wanted access to these investments to supercharge my net worth; however, you don't need to have $1 million before you start acting like an accredited investor. I bought my second investment property and started researching careers that would pay me $100,000 a year or more. I considered medicine, but ultimately decided that I would either go into finance or sales.

While working at State Farm and selling real estate on weekends, I was fortunate to meet a person who worked in the medical device industry. He worked for Johnson & Johnson and sold orthopedic implants for hips and knees – how cool! I decided that this was what I wanted to do. Over the next five years, I moved from State Farm, to Pfizer, to Johnson & Johnson, to Medtronic, the world's leading spinal and medical device company at the time. I worked hard and learned all that I could, with the goal of developing relationships, knowledge, and a skillset that I could use to develop my own business and territory. I loved the products and the people, and getting to work with surgeons was amazing.

After only two years with Medtronic, I was offered a role in Asheville, North Carolina, to take over one of the region's largest accounts. A combination of opportunity and serendipity allowed my new wife and me to move to one of our dream towns, where we began our new life and our new family. After moving into our first home, we soon found out that my wife was pregnant with our first son! As a planner, it seemed like everything was falling into place for my entire life. Then a lightning bolt ripped through my family.

In that spring, my mother was diagnosed with Stage 4 fallopian tube cancer; she had two to three years to live. She would not survive to see the birth of my second son. She wouldn't get to retire. She wouldn't get to live her dream of travelling to the National Parks in a recreational vehicle (RV). She wouldn't get to move into the home bought in Asheville with my stepfather, to be closer to her family.

After my mother passed away in December, my second son was born a week later. In the following year, I refocused my energy on becoming an investor. I wanted to guarantee the freedom to be the father and husband that I wanted to be. Less than five years later, I was able to leave my job at Medtronic so that I could devote more time to focus on real estate and take a more meaningful role in helping others.

Key Takeaways

- While high income alone does not create true wealth, it is important as the first step in the process of building your net worth. Investing in the correct financial vehicles can afford you a control over your own life that most people will never have the luxury of experiencing, which is unfortunate.

- Whether you're making $250,000 a year or $750,000 a year from your job, you may not be financially independent. The fate of your income is in the hands of others. This is a good question to ask yourself as a test: "If I were to lose my job tomorrow, would I still have streams of income, and how much would they amount to?"

- Becoming an accredited Investor gives you access to exclusive deals such as private placements, venture capital, and private equity, some of which can provide you with passive income streams. Becoming an accredited investor requires a person to demonstrate an annual income of $200,000, or $300,000 for joint income, over the previous two years with the expectation of earning the same or higher income. A person is also considered an accredited investor if that person has a net worth exceeding $1 million, either individually or jointly with their spouse.

Chapter 2

Stop Trading Time for Money — Moving From Active to Passive Income

"Is This Scalable?"

Active income is the income someone makes from his or her job, profession, small business, or personally managed investments. This can also be called "trading time for money." Active income is typically taxed at the highest rates. Most of those in the "Top 1%" mentioned by politicians will fall into this group.

As a matter of fact, the largest single profession in this Top 1% is that of physician, the same group of professionals with whom I've spent more than 15 years of my working life. I can tell you that these individuals certainly don't deserve to be vilified! Sure, some bad actors are out there, but doctors on the whole are wonderful people who spend most of their lives helping to improve the health and well-being of others. Others that fall into the top 1% group are lawyers, executives, managers, sales professionals, professional athletes, and accountants.

If you get paid by the hour, this is active income. I would consider most small business income to be active as well. If you can't walk away for a year and have your income continue to stream in, then it's not passive. I always look around my business and life and ask, "Is this scalable?" It's a concept from *The 4-Hour Workweek* by Tim Ferriss. In other words, can you get more out of the same or less effort? Active income is not scalable, while passive income is scalable.

If you can't walk away for a year and have your income continue to stream in, then it's not passive.

My goal was to get to a point of financial independence, where my passive income exceeded my basic monthly expenses: mortgage/rent, food, utilities, and insurance. This is when you can choose to live life on your own terms, which is what I wanted! If you are a high-income professional, how can you replace your active income with passive income?

3 Steps to Becoming Rich

Today I teach my young sons that investing is "money working for you." I tell them these are the steps to becoming rich:

1. **Make** money (have a high-income profession or business)

2. **Keep** money (live below your means and optimize your finances for taxation)

3. **Grow** money (become accredited and structure your portfolio for income and appreciation)

Obviously you want to get to step 3 as rapidly as possible. To do so, you need to think like an investor. One of my favorite expressions is "act as if," which means, "Act like you already are a successful investor." If you see yourself as such, the next step is to structure your accounts and portfolio so that you can automatically pour money into investments that grow year after year. Ramit Sethi does a good job of showing how to make your saving automatic with his "12-Minute Guide to Automating Your Finances."

Investing is "money working for you."

My personal rule is that I live off of 50% of my after-tax income, while saving or investing the rest. If you think about it, this formula is pretty simple. If you're saving half of what you make, for every year that you work, you can live a year on the savings. I understand that this is a pretty aggressive savings target, and for a high-income earner, a plan can work well with lower amounts as well. If you aren't able to save 50%, start with finding a way to make more money.

One of my articles posted on nextlevelincome.com discusses ways to make more time in your life, and our podcast The Next-Level Income Show has a wealth of guests who share ways to make more money and invest. Additionally, I like to structure my finances in buckets. As one fills up, it flows into the next. The way I structured my personal financial buckets can be shown using this example:

1. **Safe Bucket** (safe and liquid 6 to 24 months' worth of expenses)

2. **Protect Bucket** (life, disability, liability, health insurance)

3. **Grow Bucket** (401k, IRAs, cash, brokerage accounts, etc.)

If you are making a lot of money and you consistently save each month, eventually your excess income will flow into the third bucket. This can grow rapidly. Once you have a significant amount in your third bucket, it is time to put it to work.

What Are Your Options for Your Third Financial Bucket?

In his succinct book, *Automatic Wealth: The Six Steps to Financial Independence*, Michael Masterson outlines his thoughts on the five places where he thinks you should put your money:

1. Stocks and index funds: About 20%

2. Fixed Income: 40%-50%

3. Managed real estate: 20%-40%

4. Emergency cash and gold: 5% + 3 months' cash

5. "Play" money

It's a short read and is written from the perspective of someone who has actually become a multimillionaire, not someone who got a degree or a certification. As someone who earned an MBA in Finance and is a multimillionaire myself, I respect his advice. He outlines the reasons he likes real estate, one of which is the cash flow and returns that can be achieved in this asset class.

Richard Wilson of The Family Office Club, which works with family offices worth $100 million or more, states that these families (who have not made their money in real estate) typically devote 20% to 30% of their portfolios to income-producing real estate.

The following book is going to focus on real estate and the way I used it in my financial plan, by pouring my investment bucket into income-producing real estate, which enabled me to achieve financial independence. While I am not a financial advisor, I do have the experience of actually going through the process, making mistakes, and seeing results. I'm going to share my experience so you don't have to make the same mistakes that I did. I hope that you can use it to rapidly achieve financial freedom in your own life.

Key Takeaways

- Active income is the income you make from your job, profession, small business, or investments that you must personally manage. You can also call this "trading time for money." It's typically taxed at the highest rates and is not scalable.

- Passive income is income made from an enterprise in which the owner is not directly involved. If you can't walk away for a year while your income continues to stream in, then it's not passive. Rather than producing income through the required input of your time and effort, your invested capital is the only input required in a truly passive investment, which makes passive income scalable.

- If you desire to live life on your own terms, the practical way to achieve that lifestyle is to replace your active income with passive income.

Chapter 3

Your Opportunity Fund

I like to call the third bucket my "Opportunity Fund." When I started investing, I had a goal to invest a certain amount per year. I would pay myself first and then I would pay my essential expenses. I got to spend the leftover amount on fun things, such as travel, bikes, and more!

Personally, I like to use a concept known as "Infinite Banking", which is a specifically structured life insurance plan that allows me to build equity and then invest it when an opportunity presents itself.

Exploring Infinite Banking

Infinite Banking is a concept that was created by Nelson Nash in his book, *Becoming Your Own Banker,* which I highly recommend. Nash describes how the use of maximum overfunded whole life insurance policies that distribute dividends can allow individuals and families to control the cash flow in their lives by setting up their own "family bank" instead of relying on banks or lenders for financing.

You may have heard that whole life insurance is a bad investment, and that you should buy term life insurance and invest the rest. This is what I learned early on, even when I was working for State Farm as I finished my MBA. However, just like I discussed in the last chapter, I wanted to learn how the rich invest, not the poor or middle-class.

As I discovered, many of the wealthiest families and businesses in the world utilize whole life insurance, not only for wealth preservation, but also wealth creation.

This is a short list of some famous people you may recognize who have utilized whole life insurance to start or grow their companies:

- Walt Disney: Disney

- Ray Kroc: McDonald's

- James Cash Penney: J.C. Penney

Again, I knew that I wanted to invest like the ultra-rich, not like poor people who plan to have less money in retirement and die broke. My goal is to create multi-generational wealth. I've come to think of my life insurance policies as super-charged savings accounts. Let's look at some of the advantages and disadvantages of the infinite banking concept:

Advantages of Infinite Banking

- **Guaranteed liquidity:** You can take a loan out any time without a credit check, approval, or even giving a reason to the life insurance company!

- **Safe growth:** Certain policies have *guaranteed* cash values every year, and when you include dividends, they have historically grown by about 5%.

- **Tax efficient:** Tax-sheltered growth, tax-exempt distributions, and tax-free death benefit.

- **Annual dividend payments:** Like stocks or real estate, whole life is amazingly consistent at paying dividends every year.

- **Compounding:** There is an efficiency that is unlike anything out there, when you use the loans for investing, and create an arbitrage by paying simple interest while your equity continues to grow at a compounding rate.

Disadvantages of Infinite Banking

With the advantages above, it seems like more people would have these policies in place. However, with the advent of mutual funds over the past decades, advisors have advised clients to "buy term and invest the difference."

These are some reasons why you might not consider the infinite banking concept:

- You don't want or need a permanent death benefit.

- You can't afford the premiums or your income is not stable.

- Expenses are front-loaded; just like starting a business, there is an up-front cost to the insurance.

How to Structure Your Policy

Personally, I chose to begin our family's policies in the year when I discovered my wife was pregnant with our first son. As I made more money, I put my bonuses and extra cash into these policies and then used this cash value to buy real estate, land, and ultimately to fund partnerships when I started to syndicate deals.

The key is that you must work with an advisor who specializes in the infinite banking concept so that they can *minimize fees and maximize cash value.* An advisor who structures these policies will make a smaller commission than a typical whole life policy, and the cost of the insurance over the life of the policy is typically less than 1%. If you compare this to fees that are paid to mutual funds, fund administrators, and financial advisors, it's *significantly* less over the course of your life.

The keys to a properly structured policy are these:

- A mutual insurance company

- Whole life, dividend-paying policy

- First-year cash value of the policy should be 50% or more.

- An ideal cash value should be 70% to 80% of first-year premiums

To learn more about this strategy, visit our website at **www.nextlevelincome.com** to access a webinar and more resources.

Key Takeaways

- Infinite banking is a specifically structured life insurance plan that allows you to become your own banker by building equity and then investing it when an opportunity presents itself.

- Many of the wealthiest families and businesses in the world utilize whole life insurance, not only for wealth preservation, but also for wealth creation. It is a less frequently discussed tool of the rich.

- You can borrow against the cash value of your policy and invest it, then pay simple interest on the loan you made to yourself, while your equity continues to grow with *uninterrupted compound interest.*

Chapter 4

Why Invest in Real Estate?

During my education in portfolio management and afterward, I've learned about many different types of investments. Most of these could be called traditional investments: stocks, bonds, precious metals, and cash. Most people understand that investing in these investments is a good long-term way to build wealth. However, most don't understand how these different investments actually work.

A lot of professionals use money managers or investment advisors to help them invest. Many of these individuals are simply salespeople, but there are a lot of really good financial advisors that add significant value to their client's investment performance. Some of them even invest with us!

What are the typical components of a traditional portfolio?

The Traditional Portfolio

Cash

It's good to have three to 12 months of cash on hand for emergency expenses. Some may want more, but it's also money that is not working for you. It's also good to have some cash on hand to take advantage of investment opportunities when they arise.

Stocks

As I wrote this book, the stock market was at an all-time high, as well as the market for valuations. The "Buffett Valuation Indicator" described by Warren Buffet as "probably the best single measure of stock valuations" was at an all-time high. What does this mean? Who really knows?! The market could go significantly higher or lower in the near future.

You can buy and hold stocks, dollar-cost average into the market, day trade, buy options, and so on. There are a lot of ways to make and lose money in the stock market. It's a liquid market, which can also make it highly volatile. There are plenty of books and models describing how to incorporate stocks into a portfolio allocation.

Bonds/T-bills

Bonds are typically a complement to stocks in a diversified portfolio. Many people go by the rule that you should "have your age in percentage of bonds," so if you're 50 years old, you should have 50% of your portfolio in bonds. This may or may not be the best rule, but I'm not going to debate it here. Bonds can be in varying durations, anywhere from one year to 30 years; these can include corporate bonds and treasury bills (T-bills).

Risk, Return, and "The Holy Grail" of Investing

How do you measure expected risks and returns in a portfolio? The Sharpe Ratio, which was developed by Nobel laureate William F. Sharpe, is the average return earned in excess of the risk-free rate per unit of volatility or total risk. When subtracting the risk-free rate from the mean return, the performance associated with risk-taking activities can be isolated. One intuition of this calculation is that a portfolio engaging in zero-risk investment, such as the purchase of U.S. Treasury bills (for which the expected return is the risk-free rate), has a Sharpe ratio of exactly zero; generally, the greater the value of the Sharpe ratio, the more attractive the risk-adjusted return.

Why invest in privately held real estate as a complement to a typical 50/50 stock/bond portfolio? If you look at direct ownership of commercial real estate (see the NPI in the below graph), it had the best risk-adjusted returns compared to stocks, bonds, and REITs:

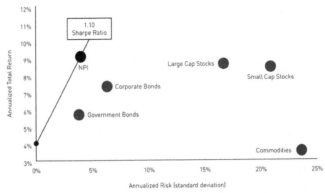

Source: Thomson Reuters Datastream; www.treasury.gov

Let's look at the effect of adding real estate to a sample portfolio. Consider Portfolio A consisting of stocks (50%), bonds (40%), and T-bills (10%).

Over a twenty-year period, this portfolio would have earned annual returns averaging 8.23%, with a standard deviation of 9.86% for a Sharpe Ratio of 0.61, as shown in the table below:

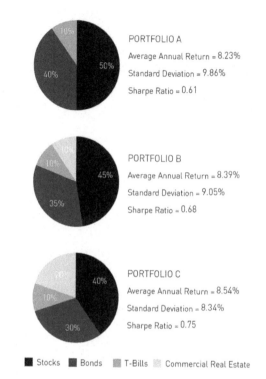

PORTFOLIO A

Average Annual Return = 8.23%

Standard Deviation = 9.86%

Sharpe Ratio = 0.61

PORTFOLIO B

Average Annual Return = 8.39%

Standard Deviation = 9.05%

Sharpe Ratio = 0.68

PORTFOLIO C

Average Annual Return = 8.54%

Standard Deviation = 8.34%

Sharpe Ratio = 0.75

■ Stocks ■ Bonds ■ T-Bills ▨ Commercial Real Estate

Data from 1995-2014. The indices used for each asset class are: S&P 500; Barclay's U.S. Aggregate (Bonds); Bank of America/Merrill Lynch 3-month U.S. Treasury Bill; and NCREIF NPI (CRE).

By investing 20% of the portfolio in real estate, while reducing exposure to stocks and bonds, this portfolio could have achieved higher risk-adjusted returns as shown in Portfolio C and a higher Sharpe Ratio of 0.75. This reflects a 23% increase in return versus risk! Ray Dalio, by some measurements a more successful investor than Warren Buffet, calls increased return with decreased risk "The Holy Grail" of investing.

As a direct owner of commercial real estate, you would be allowed to increase your return and decrease the risk of your portfolio

"Working in wealth management, offering products to invest directly into commercial real estate, has been essential to build a proper asset allocation for my clients. Not only does commercial real estate provide the opportunity for me to get my clients more attractive after-tax income compared to using only stocks and bonds, but the low correlation with other asset classes helps to reduce the overall risk while increasing portfolio return. For me this is a complete necessity!"

— Nick, Wealth Manager; Montreal, Canada

What is important to note is that NPI (the National Council of Real Estate Investment Fiduciaries Property Index) is classified as properties that are income-producing. What this means is that their value is largely based on the net operating income that they produce, not the comparable sales method.

Before diving deeper into this different methodology, beyond what most people are used to in valuing real estate, let's look at some other areas spread across the real estate investing spectrum.

Key Takeaways

- Traditional investments follow the traditional notion of low-risk yielding low returns, and high risks yielding potentially higher returns, but with a greater possibility of losing money on the investment.

- The "holy grail" of investing is increased return with decreased risk. This is not typical of most types of investments.

- Privately held commercial real estate on its own has an attractive Sharpe ratio, or risk-adjusted return. If you add commercial real estate to a traditional portfolio comprised of stocks, bonds, and T-bills, it can increase your portfolio's potential of high returns while simultaneously decreasing overall risk.

Chapter 5

Overview of Common Real Estate Investments

Perhaps you've read this far because you want to be an investor, and you feel that real estate can benefit your portfolio. You're probably thinking, "What are my options?" Over the past 20 years, I have invested in nearly every type of real estate.

This includes:

- REITs (Real Estate Investment Trusts)

- Private Lending

- Performing & non-performing notes

- Development

- Commercial: multifamily, office, storage

- Single-family rentals (Buy & Hold)

- Short-term/Vacation rentals

About the only area where I haven't invested is in the hotel industry. However, I've spent considerable time investigating this space.

Some Options and Lessons Learned

Real Estate Investment Trusts (REITs)

REITs are essentially real-estate-flavored mutual funds. This is the easiest way to get exposure to real estate, since they have low or no minimum investment levels. They must invest at least 75% of the total assets in real estate, cash, or U.S. Treasuries, and then pay 90% or more of its taxable income in the form of shareholder dividends each year.

While REITs allow for diversification of a portfolio, they are also highly correlated to the stock market due to their liquidity, and the fact that when investors sell stocks, they often sell REIT shares along with them. The following chart shows the risk or volatility levels across stocks and REITs compared to Directly Owned Real Estate (NCREIF):

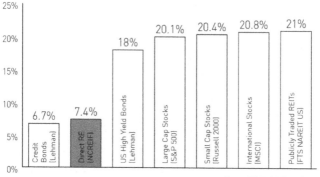

Source: KBS Capital Market Group

Private Lending

Private lending is another way to get a return from real estate without actually owning and managing real estate. However, you must have a solid understanding of valuing and operating properties to be successful in this space. You underwrite properties or deals and lend money to investors based upon the underlying value of the asset.

Alternatively, you can pay someone else a fee — usually around 20% of the return —

to do this. Sometimes called hard money loans or trust deeds, this is a way to get interest payments on a regular basis, and receive your principal back at the end of the loan term.

At Next-Level Income, we have had several successful loans and a few unsuccessful ones. If a loan defaults you need to be comfortable taking back the property, renting it, or rehabbing it and selling it to recoup your investment. Some investors actually enjoy taking properties back when loans default. These individuals are often experienced fix-and-flippers or contractors themselves.

Non-Performing Notes

This brings us to performing and non-performing notes. Performing notes are those notes that are purchased from lenders that have originated the loans. It's one step removed from private lending. Non-performing notes are just that: notes that aren't paying. Typically these are bought in large pools at a deep discount to mitigate the high default rates.

Why would you want to buy these? I can say from experience that if you can get these notes performing again you can get very good returns. However, the process takes a lot of time and you need to account for loans being written off as worthless. Really, this is a business bringing in active income. There are entire books and seminars about this sector.

Development

My wife is an architect. After the real estate market stabilized in 2012, we began a development company; we bought lots, she designed the homes, and then we hired a builder to construct spec homes before we sold them. Again, this area of real estate is truly a business; the profits that you make are typically taxed as regular income. The homes are called "spec homes" because you are making a speculative play on the price of the home when it is time to sell.

The time from purchase of a piece of property to sale is typically 12 to 18 months. You'll need to plan on getting financing from a bank or private lender, or financing the build yourself.

If you are not a general contractor, then you will need to hire one, as well as hire an architect to design a desirable and cost-effective layout. Then you'll need to find a realtor to market and sell the property. While it's possible to make good returns in this space, at Next-Level Income we are not currently doing development deals, due to the shrinking margins and higher comparative risk involved in this area.

Office/Industrial

Another area where I've invested is commercial office space. The commercial market typically lags behind the residential market because the business cycle follows net migration patterns in an area. Just like in residential, you purchase a property and rent out the space, but instead of residents there are business tenants. Typical leases are one to five years and incorporate a base rent plus expenses. We have a property with multiple tenants, which means we not only need to keep up with the various tenants and lengths of their leases, but also the various upfits for each space and allocations for capital for improvements that may need to be made.

Industrial leases can be another option in the "office" arena where investors can get long-term leases with businesses that rent out large warehouses and the like. (I have also invested in self-storage units, which are another segment of this space, but also have characteristics similar to multifamily.)

Office and industrial real estate can be a profitable area, but there are particular nuances when it comes to macro and micro-business cycles. Everything from the local economy to national trade policies can have large effects on this space. Investors need to work with an expert who understands this as well as the management side.

Short-term/Vacation Rentals

We live in Asheville, North Carolina, which is a major tourist destination. We use one of our properties as a hybrid rental/guest house. I also have several friends that have done very well in this area. However, I wouldn't recommend this area for a passive investor. The main reason is that this area is very time-intensive if you self-manage and typically it has some of the highest management fees in real estate. Like development, it's more of a business. With management fees often as high as 25% to 40%, your total operating expenses in this area can be as high as 75% of gross rents.

Single-Family Rentals (1-4 units)

I got started as a real estate investor in single-family rentals, including houses, townhouses, condominiums, etc. This is a space that is familiar to almost everyone and it is one of the easiest to get started. For instance, you can just rent a room to someone else, and boom! You're a landlord!

Owning rental homes is a great way to get started if you have a small amount of money to invest and don't mind being a landlord, or have a partner who will handle all of this for you. I was on call for more than 10 years of my life, and it's similar if you are managing your own properties; you always need to be prepared to get a phone call with an issue. My wife could talk about me taking a phone call at a Costa Rican resort during our honeymoon to deal with an urgent tenant issue. That being said, buying a single-family home and renting was the easiest way for me to get started as a real estate investor as a 21-year-old college kid.

A popular strategy, which was once my own, is to buy multiple properties and eventually pay off the mortgages until you get to keep the cash flow from rentals after taxes, insurance, property management fees, repairs, etc. Typical net proceeds from rentals are around 60% to 70%, assuming that you are paying a 10% management fee, average taxes, and keeping reserves of about 10% for maintenance, repairs, and vacancies.

As a general rule of thumb, you should expect to get about 1% of the purchase price for monthly rent. So if you buy a home for $150,000, you need to get about $1,500 per month in rent. If you can buy 10 houses over the course of 5 years with 20% down, and then pay off the mortgages over the next 10 years or quicker, you would bring in a gross amount of about $15,000 per month and net of around $10,000 month. This was my original plan.

What I found about 10 years into my fifteen-year plan was that my original 30%+ return on my investment had dropped to around 7%. Even worse was that as a high-income earner I had lost most of my tax benefits, which meant I was netting less than 5% on my equity after taxes. You don't need a degree in finance to know that you can do better than that kind of return!

In addition, I was tired of dealing with the headaches of managing multiple properties, even though I had property managers in place. I had to approve repairs, new tenants, pay for vacancies every year, and deal with staff turnover within my management companies. As a busy professional with two young children, the last thing I wanted to do was to deal with these issues on my personal time.

So, where do I invest now? Read on to find out.

Key Takeaways

- Most types of real estate investments end up being active investments rather than passive investments, requiring the input of additional ongoing time and effort after the initial acquisition.

- As a high-income earner, much of your returns on certain real estate investments can be eaten away in taxes because you will be required to pay the highest tax rate on your income earned from the investment.

- Many of these areas of real estate are correlated with both micro and macro-economic cycles. If a negative event happens on either level, there is the likelihood that it may have an impact on your investment.

Chapter 6

The Holy Grail

While at a business planning meeting with my wife in 2012, I was lamenting the performance of my real estate portfolio to a gentlemen, who suggested that I look into the multifamily space. As an open-minded person who is always looking for improvements in my financial life, I reached out to some syndicators in the apartment space. I interviewed them on their operations, markets, and the benefits of being an investor.

What I discovered were three key differences between owning residential properties and multifamily properties:

1. **Being an investor is 100% passive;** you have an *asset manager* who handles all of the day-to-day aspects of the investment. This means no more phone calls while on vacation to deal with a bad tenant or a broken appliance!

2. **High-income investors retain the tax benefits of owning real estate,** which means better after-tax returns. (Please note that I am not a CPA and every person's tax situation is unique.)

3. **Your investment returns SCALE.** Instead of returns eroding over time as they do with residential real estate, an investment in the multifamily space can continue to grow at double-digit rates due to its unique characteristics compared to residential real estate.

As a bonus, the debt is non-recourse. What does this mean? The loan is secured by the property, not by personal guarantees. For high net worth investors, this can often be the most important difference in asset classes.

Over the next three years, I sold all of my residential properties and moved our equity into commercial multifamily properties. The benefits I received were not only less hassles and management, but also higher returns and lower taxes, which ultimately meant we were keeping more money with less work!

"I've worked with Chris and his wife since they have been investing in apartments. As a CPA for multiple high net worth individuals, the value in properly structured commercial real estate is that it's not only passive but the income and proceeds are tax-advantaged. Many of my clients benefit from having real estate as part of their overall financial picture."

— Bret, CPA; North Carolina

Why exactly did I do this? I previously quoted from Ray Dalio, the most successful hedge fund investor of all time who also manages the largest hedge fund in the world. He calls the combination of reducing risks while increasing returns "The Holy Grail." I felt like I found the Holy Grail when I discovered the multifamily space. I could get the returns that I was looking for while being a passive investor, maintaining tax benefits, and not having to change my strategy as my portfolio grew.

Let's take a deeper look into each area of returns from this space as well as some of the tax benefits as well.

Income Is the Outcome

Owning an apartment building really means owning a business that just happens to be real estate. Why is this so great? Good businesses produce cash flow. If you are a business owner, then you know that cash flow is the lifeblood of sustaining and growing your business. Financial independence is the same. If you think about your life as a business, you need regular cash flow to support your lifestyle.

My definition of financial independence is having enough passive cash flow to pay for the lifestyle that I choose to live. For some this may be covering the basic necessities such as rent, groceries, insurance and car payments.

Others may define it as two homes paid off and enough money to travel regularly.

Once you decide on your lifestyle, you need an income to support it. Your investments should enable you to do that. Otherwise you will need to draw down your principal over time to support your lifestyle.

My definition of financial independence is having enough passive cash flow to pay for the lifestyle that I choose to live.

This is where the financial experts' 4% Rule applies. It states that you can withdraw 4% of your portfolio every year in retirement. The problem is that in recent years, this number has failed 50% of the time[1]. This has led some experts to conclude that 3% is the new safe withdrawal rate (SWR). So if you need $100,000 per year to be financially

---

[1] Tergesen, A. (2018, February 9). *Forget the 4% Rule: Rethinking Common Retirement Beliefs*. Retrieved from https://www.wsj.com

independent, you would need about $3.3 million in savings and investments versus the $2.5 million under the 4% rule.

"I've known Chris personally and professionally for several years and have been an investor in every property. As a 'high income professional' I'm looking for passive investments that are stable and will eventually supplement and replace my income as a surgeon. I'm thankful to have been introduced to the space and hope that I can help to introduce others to this area of real estate."

— Marc, Orthopedic Surgeon, North Carolina

When properly structured, commercial real estate (multifamily to be more specific), can provide tax-advantaged income to investors. This means you get cash flow that you can actually spend.

Controlled Appreciation

Picture a rollercoaster. Do you feel fear or dread? Personally I enjoy riding rollercoasters, but not when it's my money taking a ride. I felt like my real estate portfolio was on a rollercoaster from 2000 to 2013 and you can see why when looking at this chart of home prices:

S&P/Case-Shiller U.S. National Home Price Index

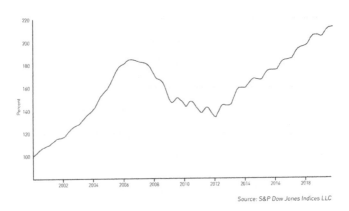

Source: S&P Dow Jones Indices LLC

My portfolio value rose rapidly, fell back down, and then rose back up again. In retrospect, I still feel that hanging on for the long run was the best thing, but I yearned for a way to avoid that feeling again.

Multifamily real estate has something I like to call "controlled appreciation."

You might think, "If I buy a property and the market goes up, that's appreciation." You would be correct, but your home is valued on something called comparable sales. If your neighbor's house sells for $200 per square foot, chances are that your house is worth about $200 per square foot. How does valuation work in commercial real estate? That's right; it's the same income that we just finished reviewing in the previous section.

The next chapter dives deeper into income and value and how they grow, but this is an example of how you would value a 100-unit property using Net Operating Income (NOI) and the cap rate. A definition of NOI is total revenue minus all other expenses. The cap rate is the rate of return on a property based on the income the property is expected to generate.

100-unit property
NOI: $600,000
Cap rate: 6.0%
Value = $600,000 ÷ 6.0% = **$10,000,000**

If income is increased by $100 per unit, what does that do to the value?
NOI increase = $100 x 100 units
x 12 months = $120,000
New NOI: $720,000
Cap rate: 6.0%
Value = $720,000 ÷ 6.0% = **$12,000,000**

Increasing rents by just $100 per month allows you to increase the value of the property by 20%. If you had a $4 million investment in this property, you've created a 50% increase in your equity through a $100 per unit rental increase.

Now this is a very simple example. There are a lot of variables and work that goes into creating a $100 increase in net rents in a property; however, you can see how the controllable differences in income have a real effect on value. The difference between what I used to do (buy, rent, and hope) is vastly different from my current work with improving properties and income to materially affect value.

In addition, because multifamily real estate is valued based on income, it is not correlated to the overall market that includes stocks, residential housing market, and so on, which further reduces your risk and exposure.

The Principle of It All

Do you have a mortgage? Look at your last statement; chances are that a portion of your monthly payment goes to principal. In a large multifamily property, typically another 1% to 3% every year adds to your equity buildup in the property. The income from the property goes toward what is called "debt service," or the mortgage on the property. It's not sexy or exciting, but predictable. Since your investment is leveraged, a 1% increase in equity may equal a 2% to 3% increase in your annual returns.

Non-Recourse Debt

Remember that typically the debt on stable, well-performing, multifamily assets is non-recourse. This means that the lender uses the property as collateral on the loan, not the owner's or investor's personal guarantee. If a bank reclaims a property with non-recourse debt, the investors may lose their investment but they aren't personally liable for the original loan.

This is not the case with your typical residential property. I know several people who either went bankrupt during 2008 to 2009 or who are still paying off bad loans 10 years later, due to recourse debt. As your net worth increases, this is probably something that you would weight more heavily.

What's the Net?

(Please note that I am not a CPA. and you should consult a tax professional to review your personal tax situation.)

If you're reading this, chances are that you're a high-income earner. If you're an accredited investor, then you may not be getting all of the tax benefits offered by real estate.

If you made more than $326,000 as a married couple in 2020, your marginal tax rate would look something like this:

Federal Tax: 32%
State/Local: 7% (median rate for the U.S.)
Total = 39%

Most likely, you will be paying FICA (Social Security, Medicare, etc.) in addition to other taxes. For simplicity, let's use a marginal tax rate of 40%. Your actual rate is likely higher or lower.

NOTE: If you live in a state like California, you may be paying as much as 50% in combined taxes! I have many friends that live in California paying more than 40% of their income in taxes.

Let's say your target after-tax rate of return is 12%. What level rate of return do you have to earn before taxes to meet your target? At a 40% marginal rate, you need to be earning 20% returns or greater. Now that is possible in the world of real estate; however, in my experience, rates like this have come from riskier or more active investments like vacation rentals, non-performing notes, development, etc.

Again, in my experience, none of these options can capture all of the great tax benefits provided by real estate. To do so you need to offset cash flow and gains with depreciation, a type of "phantom expense."

Phantom Expenses

What is a phantom expense? Phantom expenses decrease your taxable income but don't decrease your cash flow. Our favorite is depreciation. The reason is that deprecation can offset much (if not all) of the income from a property, thus enhancing after-tax returns.

The tax code allows you to use depreciation, or cost recovery, to write off the value of the physical structures that make up your property (but not the land it's on) over time. The time period of depreciation for residential buildings such as apartments is currently set at 27.5 years.

So if you have a $12 million property, and you determine that the physical structures are worth $10 million, your depreciation allowance for each year will look something like this:

$10M/27.5 years = $363,636

Now that is an attractive deduction! Savvy investors who are looking for a shorter hold period, somewhere between three and seven years, can take it even further by utilizing cost segregation to identify and accelerate depreciation on short-life property. This acceleration of the depreciation increases the allowance, which in turn increases cash flow and further reduces the tax burden during the projected hold period. Investors generally aim at a hold period of three to seven years and use depreciation to its fullest extent.

"I progressed from owning a rental house, to owning a quadruplex, to investing in multifamily residential. The net effect has been better returns, much lower taxes, and no more headaches. Living in a very high tax state makes the tax reduction very welcome indeed."

— David, Retired; California

Key Takeaways

- Multifamily is the "holy grail" of real estate investing. Your investment is 100% passive with an asset manager handling the day-to-day issues, while the tax treatment allows you to keep most (if not all) of the income generated by the property, and the debt is non-recourse.

- Apartments are valued like a business, rather than by comparable sales like houses. Because of this, you're able to grow a property's value by improving the NOI of the property, a process I like to call "controlled appreciation." In addition, because multifamily real estate is valued based on income, it is not correlated to the overall market (stocks, residential housing market, etc.), which further reduces your risk and exposure.

- The unique combination of attributes provided by multifamily real estate will make it an attractive investment vehicle for high-income earners.

Chapter 7

"The Rising Tide" — Multifamily Fundamentals

"A rising tide lifts all boats."
— John F. Kennedy

As I did my due diligence on the multifamily space, I discovered what I call "The Rising Tide." After the real estate crash and Great Recession, home ownership tumbled from a high of 69% in 2006 to 63.7%, and it continues to hover around 65% today.

Homeownership Rate for the United States

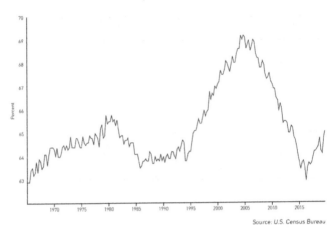

Source: U.S. Census Bureau

The Four Trends

Renting has increased sharply across most age groups:

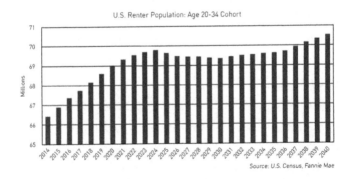

Source: U.S. Census, Fannie Mae

What are the reasons for this?

Trend 1: Millennials

Over the next decade, the number of millennial renter households will double from its current number of 11.3 million to 22.6 million households. For lifecycle reasons, young adults of all generations have always tended to have less income and less wealth, making them more inclined to rent rather than to own. But in the wake of the Great Recession of 2007 to 2009, a slack labor market, record student debt, and reduced access to forms of credit and mortgages have exacerbated this tendency. In some metros, nearly one in five millennials expect to rent *forever*.

Trend 2: Growing Minority and Immigrant Population

While the latest political cycle included a lot of talk about immigration, the fact remains that immigrants will be the largest demographic of renters growing from 33.9 million in 2015 to 38.5 million in 2035. Immigrants also tend to rent in greater proportions than those reflected by our current population.

The minority population in the United States will account for approximately 75% of household growth in the coming decade. This influx will continue to contribute to the growing share of minority households in America. Primarily for economic reasons, minorities and immigrants are more likely to rent than anyone in Caucasian households born in the United States. Research by the Joint Center for Housing Studies indicates that about half of all immigrants to the United States are renters, including 74% of immigrants under age 35.

Trend 3: Baby Boomers

U.S. Census Bureau statistics revealed that, between 2007 and 2017, the biggest changes in the renting population came from seniors aged 60 and over. This shows an increase of 43%, compared to only a 7% increase in renters aged 34 or younger.

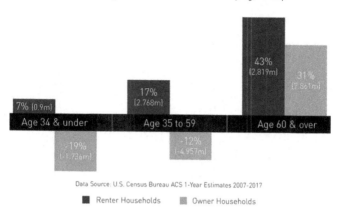

Data Source: U.S. Census Bureau ACS 1-Year Estimates 2007-2017

■ Renter Households   ▨ Owner Households

A **CNBC article** shared interviews with baby boomers that offered a similar perspective to the millennials of preferring rentals for both economic and lifestyle reasons. ("Baby Boomers, Like Millennials, are Flocking to Rentals Offering a 'Hands-Free' Lifestyle", CNBC, 11/25/17)

One boomer shared, "As you get older, there are only so many things you want to concentrate on. Apartment life lets you focus on things that matter and get rid of stuff that takes up a lot of time." Well said!

Trend 4: High-Income Renters

Another interesting trend of 2019 is that not only are those renters in the median income range ($40,100 for an individual to $63,030 for a household), but also the majority of growth in renters is coming from high-income households.

Some may think that owning apartments means being a slumlord, but in reality many renters choose to rent and appreciate being in a safe, clean neighborhood near good jobs and schools. Understanding this trend and focusing on markets with strong demographics, good jobs, and schools can help drive performance of an asset.

Supply and Demand

Currently, people are more likely to rent; that trend will continue over the next decade and across all age groups. Where will they live? A study by the National Multifamily Housing Council states that the U.S. needs 4.6 million new apartments by 2030.

Some highlights from the research:

- More than 75 million people between 18 and 34 years old are entering the housing market, primarily as renters.

- The Western U.S. and the Southeast are expected to have the greatest need for new apartment housing through 2030.

- It will take an average of at least 328,000 new apartment homes built every year to meet demand; yet on average, just 255,000 apartments were delivered from 2011 to 2018.

As these new renters enter the market, some will want to live in the latest and greatest properties, though it's already known that there are not enough. In addition, the individual income in the U.S. in 2019 was about $40,100 and $63,030 for a household. Assuming that a household devotes 25% of their budget to housing, they are looking at a range of about $800 to $1,200 per month for budgeted rent. At an average rent of around $1,000, a typical renter will be unable to afford a new luxury building in the hot area of downtown; however, they will want to live in a clean, safe neighborhood with good schools.

Supplying this type of demand is challenging, but possible with the right strategy.

Creating Value

How do you create value for the residents in this space? At Next-Level Income, we employ something called a value-add strategy. We acquire assets in growing submarkets where we can deploy capital for improvements while improving operations. Our goal is to purchase properties built within the last 30 years that require $5,000 to $10,000 per unit to improve. So for a $15 million property that requires around $4 million in down payment, we may raise another $2 million for improvements, along with reserves.

Why would we want to spend so much on improvements? These improvements create demand from those same residents who want to live in a nice neighborhood but they can't spend $1,500 or more per month to rent. However, these same residents may be able to afford $1,000 or $1,200 per month. Our residents are generally given the option of an affordable unit, since we don't kick out paying residents, or a newly upgraded unit so they can stay in the neighborhood where they've come to call home.

Turning $1 into $17

One of the things we love about the space is something called "controlled appreciation."

For example, perhaps we spend $7,500 on a unit that is currently renting for $900 per month. We may add wood flooring, new appliances, new paint, cabinet finishes, new hardware, and fixtures. This unit may now rent for $1,050 or another $150 per month, totaling $1,800 per year. In the commercial real estate market, the properties are not valued on comparable sales as are residential properties. They are valued on income and market cap rates as described in the previous chapter.

If a property is sold or bought at a 6% cap rate, or a value that is the equivalent of paying the price that equals the amount of income divided by 6%, every dollar saved or grown as income turns into almost $17.

This is the math:

> Income: $900,000
> Cap rate: 6%
> Value = $900,000 at 6% = $15,000,000

If we take that math into account, the $1,800 created in the above example now equals $30,000 in appreciation of the property. Now multiply that number by 200 units...

Getting excited yet? Let's take a deeper look at the numbers, as well as ways to select the right properties and create value for our investors.

Key Takeaways

- Demographic trends of steadily decreasing homeownership rates and an ever-increasing renter population across all age groups (especially millennials and baby boomers) are a key factor in the continuous growth multifamily demand.

- Demand for multifamily units is greater than the supply of units and will continue to increase for years to come.

- A value-add approach to multifamily real estate investment allows investors to control the appreciation of a property by acquiring "the worst house in the best neighborhood," improving it, then increasing revenue through rent growth while decreasing expenses through efficiencies. These measures will improve NOI and grow the overall value of the property.

Chapter 8

Diamonds in the Rough — Market Analysis and Acquiring Deals

I trained as an engineer in school; it involves a lot of detail. While training for bike racing, I focused on small details every single day, using data to achieve a higher level of performance, with long-term goals planned out for years. I do the exact same thing with deals and personal wealth, using data and analytical training as well as a top-down approach to markets before I even consider buying a property. This is called the "Engineering Design Process."

Market Selection and Analysis

When an investor sent me a deal that was in a tertiary market and wanted to get my thoughts, I told him that I wasn't interested. He said, "But you haven't even seen the deal yet!" How did I make that decision before looking at the numbers? I got there because I already knew the market.

At Next-Level Income, we don't consider a property to purchase before we thoroughly analyze a market and decide that it hits all the right metrics in our detailed analysis of more than two dozen metrics. These include total population and growth, employment figures, rents, cap rates, and transaction volume. After all, if you buy a property and the market isn't good, you can't physically move your apartment building to a better market.

Establish Insider Relationships

After analyzing a market and deciding that it fits all of our criteria, the next thing to do is build a local team and network. This is perhaps the hardest and most arduous part of what we do. It takes time up front and is an ongoing process.

Deal Analysis

Once we've developed a network of brokers and owner relationships, met with lenders, and have chosen one or two top property management companies in the Metropolitan Statistical Area (MSA), we are now ready to start our deal analysis. A spreadsheet will cover an entire wall in my office, where we enter numbers such as current expenses, rents, rent growth, closing costs, and expected improvements.

These are all key assumptions; the greater their accuracy, the better our decision making process can be. We know that if the assumptions are incorrect, the conclusion is incorrect. Not only do we independently analyze these numbers, but also we consult with our management team and lender while continuing to underwrite a deal. As we consider acquisition of a property, we may look at 10 to 20 deals a week and underwrite several of them.

When a property meets our stringent underwriting criteria, typically less than 10 out of 100, we will consider making an offer on a property. This is done with a Letter of Intent (LOI) that details our offer and initial terms. This often includes hundreds of thousands of dollars of deposits and earnest money on a multimillion-dollar property. You can see why we want to be sure that the numbers work before laying down six figures in deposits that may be lost if we don't close on a property!

Prospective sellers want real assurance that a buyer can get the deal done. It's often not enough just to offer the right purchase price. The terms need to be solid, and you need to have credibility with brokers and sellers. Either you can have cash in hand, or gain backing from lenders such as Fannie Mae and Freddie Mac. Typically offers move into a "best and final" phase before being accepted.

This is one of the most frustrating aspects of what we do. After performing weeks of analysis, touring properties, and consulting with our lenders, then we lose a deal to another buyer. While you don't want to overpay, you also don't want to lose out to another buyer on a property because you got the numbers right, but you didn't have credibility or offer the right terms. Clearly it's a fine line. It's also the most exciting and nervous time during the life cycle of a property!

Due Diligence

Prior to sending a formal offer, we are on site with our property management team and lender. We want to be sure that what we see on paper can be verified in person. Once we have an executed contract, that's when the excitement begins. We begin scheduling tours to walk through every unit and consider when to rate-lock; then we start moving money into deposit accounts and writing checks. Our local property management team and lenders all continue to participate right alongside us.

"Since joining First Communities Management in 1988 I've had the pleasure of working with many individual owners, operators, and investors in the multifamily space. The keys to success lie in a thorough due diligence, developing operational efficiencies and building relationships. Chris understands the value in multifamily but also how to create more value

through pulling the levers that improve communities and improve operating income."

— Ed Romano, Executive VP First Communities Management; Georgia

The due diligence process gets underway immediately, and typically it continues for 30 to 60 days. This is the time for us to confirm our assumptions. We may adjust the numbers in our analysis during this time to make sure that we can still achieve the financial results that we projected, as our investors also expect. If we see something that seriously changes in our analysis, we may choose not to purchase a property during this time.

One example of this occurred during due diligence on a property as we did a thorough lease audit. We discovered that a large percentage of the renters were from a local school. We contacted the school and discovered that it was building its own housing facility and was not planning to renew the leases. We chose not to move forward with the purchase. In most cases, we confirm our assumptions during due diligence and move toward closing.

Once we own a property, we must begin to execute our plan efficiently. Like so many things in life and business, getting the right people in place is essential for long-term success in the multifamily space. Let's look into each member of our team and the roles they play.

Key Takeaways

- Market selection or MSA is the key first step in multifamily real estate investing. You must make sure the market currently holds and will continue to show the necessary characteristics for success in the multifamily space. Remember, the multifamily market is fueled by population growth and employment growth. If you buy a property in a poor market, you can't move your apartment building to another area.

- Once you've selected the market where you'd like to find deals, the next step is to establish relationships with key insiders in that market, such as brokers, owners, and property managers. Many of the best deals happen off-market and you'll never get a chance to see them if you don't have these relationships.

- Now that you've established the necessary relationships, you can begin analyzing potential deals. Get your spreadsheets ready. To give some perspective, due to our stringent underwriting criteria we will typically only make an offer on less than 10 out of every 100 potential deals we analyze. And that's before the due diligence period, the results of which may remove the deal from our consideration as well.

- The due diligence period is the time to confirm your assumptions. No stone left unturned is the only way to go, and it is the approach taken by our team. Once this period is completed and you own the property, any problem experienced by the previous owner becomes your problem. Be willing to walk away from a bad deal. Do not make the mistake of letting costs you've already sunk into it persuade you to go through with it.

Chapter 9

Real Estate Is a Team Sport

Most people who are not familiar with cycling don't realize that it is a team sport. While individuals tend to get all of the glory, you need a team to support the star rider(s) so that they can execute when the time is right. The field of real estate is similar. You need to have a competent team that you trust, not only so they can bring you opportunities, but also to help execute initiatives once you are an owner.

At this point, it's all about managing people and making sure that everyone is executing in their role. As we enter a market, we begin to build a team prior to analyzing and looking at deals.

Team Members

Market Analyst

The junior member of our team is used to screen deals, to see if they pass our initial criteria for a market.

- Is the deal too big or too small?

- Is it too old or too new?

- Is it on the wrong side of the tracks?

- How is the neighborhood for crime and schools?

- Is the area on the way up or down?

We don't necessarily want to own the best property in a neighborhood. An analyst can screen all of these data points for you to determine if a property should advance to underwriting.

Brokers

Not only do you need to know all of the top brokers in your target markets, but they also have to know you. They need to know you're credible, have closed on other deals, and areas where your money is coming from (investors, 1031 exchange or your own capital). Sometimes we develop ongoing relationships with brokers years before we purchase a property in a market. We spend time looking at deals, touring properties, and regularly reviewing markets and activity with our team.

"I have seen from hosting 30+ investor relations workshops and meeting with well over 1,000 single family offices regarding their direct investments that the group with the exclusive deal flow, better valuation deals, those who see the first deals, or those who see the most deal flow overall win. There is a compound effect that occurs when you get to see and close deals before anyone else knew they were available, and when you can be strategically helpful to an asset long-term, that is more likely to happen at market rates or at discounted rates due to your superior strategic value. We have found for those on the sell and buy side that putting in place deal flow multipliers, positioning yourself to be found often by those prospects with assets, and making it crystal clear to everyone your team interacts with exactly what your unique focus is can allow you to consistently attract more deal flow and in turn produce better results consistently. We look at it as a totem

pole of deal flow; if you only see 50 deals a year, your top 10% of deals is just 5 deals, but if you see 200 deals you have 20 to select from and you can stack them against each other to compare opportunities, see true market value faster, and have more conviction committing to closing deals that you are more certain are a market anomaly where you can create value. In short, as long as quality is kept high and there is focus, more deal flow is better than less."

— Richard Wilson, The Family Office Club; Florida

Lenders

A strong lending team will not only help you to get funding, but also help to underwrite deals. They will help you to source the appropriate debt for a deal, and they are critically important during the underwriting process, as they will confirm what our team has concluded. In addition, a lender can help be an equity matchmaker or even be a referral to owners looking to sell other properties. Lenders are obviously a critical component of our team.

Property Manager

Once we own a property, the property management team is truly our "boots on the ground". The importance of this piece of your team can't be overstated. We are in communication with our property managers on a weekly or even daily basis as we staff our properties, execute our value-add strategies, source vendors and contractors, and continuously analyze market rents and trends in the communities. Since resident turnover can reach as high as 50%, a property manager can literally make or break the performance of a property. Being involved with a bad property manager can be like being in a bad marriage; separating can be ugly, costly, and lengthy. We are fortunate to work with top regional management companies and don't take this for granted.

Attorneys

From due diligence to ownership, a team of attorneys is necessary to help navigate the legal seas. A local real estate attorney is needed in each market to handle the transaction. A general business attorney and SEC attorney are also needed for syndication matters. Trusted advisors in this area can save a lot of time and future heartache.

Tax Advisors/CPAs

We are not CPAs and don't pretend to be. However, we spend a lot of time considering and discussing taxes and the great treatment of real estate under IRS code. One of the benefits of real estate is depreciation. A firm that specializes in Cost Segregation Analysis is critically important to help maximize the impact of depreciation. In addition, a CPA is needed to prepare personal returns as well as a firm that specializes in partnerships, if other investors are involved.

If you are doing a 1031 exchange, your team will also need an intermediary to structure the transaction properly. Considering that taxes can be your biggest personal expense, and in a property every additional dollar of taxes saved goes directly to our bottom line, we absolutely depend on (and love) our tax team. Since property taxes are one of our largest expenses, we also utilize a local firm to manage and contest our property tax bill when appropriate.

Asset Manager

Who will manage the managers? The role of asset manager is to oversee operations on a regular (often daily) basis, manage capital expenditures, evaluate liquidity strategies, all with the sole purpose of protecting investor's capital and maximizing returns. Ray Alcorn knew this when he told me to learn about property management over 20 years ago. In this role you need to understand how each piece of the team works. An asset manager's job is to make sure every decision is made in the best interest of investors.

Remember, real estate is a team sport. You must continually work with, develop, and sometimes change your team to make sure that they are optimizing the performance of your asset.

Key Takeaways

- You need a solid team to bring you potential opportunities and help you execute as an owner.

- Your reputation is everything. Cultivating relationships and your reputation across markets will enable you to maintain and grow your deal flow.

- Prospective sellers want assurance that a buyer can get the deal done. It's not enough just to offer a great purchase price. The terms must be solid and you need to have credibility with brokers and sellers; either you should have cash in hand, or backing from lenders such as Fannie Mae and Freddie Mac.

Chapter 10

Multi-Generational Wealth

"Working hard for something we don't care about is called stress. Working hard for something we love is called passion."
— Simon Sinek

Chances are that you have not read this book just to make more money or better returns. You want to have more options and opportunities for freedom that money offers. The goal of investing shouldn't be just the money.

I love my family. I love spending time with them. I love being outside in the mountains. I love having the freedom to help other people. What is your "Why" in relation to investing?

- Are you investing to escape your current job?

- Are you investing to provide a way to replace your income for retirement?

- Are you investing to pay for your children's education?

Whatever is the answer, your investment plan should help to facilitate that.

After working to grow my family's net worth I want to be sure that I can create true, lasting wealth for them. One of the great advantages of real estate is the ability to utilize a 1031 or Starker Exchange to create lasting wealth. Section 1031 of the IRS code allows you to sell a property and use the proceeds to buy a "like kind" property. Then you can defer taxes indefinitely. Yes, you read that correctly: indefinitely.

Let's look at the impact this can have over a twenty-year period:

- Initial investment: $100,000

- Average investment life cycle: 5 years

- Average return 12%

- Investment at year 5, 10, and 15: $181,670, $330,039, and $599,580

- After taxes (20% long-term capital gains rate): $145,336, $211,225, and $306,985

- After-tax value at year 20: $446,159

- Value at year 20 utilizing tax-deferred exchanges: $1,089,255

That's nearly 2.5X the value over a twenty-year period due to tax deferral!

As someone who's utilized the 1031 Exchange to great effect, I can attest to its utility and power. Over the course of 20 years, I was able to transform an initial $3,000 investment into a $3,000-per-month cash flow and $400,000 in equity through use of a 1031 exchange. I did not pay tax on the cash flow or capital gains due to proper tax structure.

It is equally as powerful when you structure properly, that you can transfer property to your heirs at a stepped-up basis. Of course, you should consult an estate-planning attorney to address your personal situation.

You can see the power of this strategy when utilized along with the 1031 exchange over the course of an investor's life. My goal is not only to build wealth, but also to teach my children to be wealthy, and help others to do the same.

Key Takeaways

- Investing your money in multifamily real estate gives you the option to defer your capital gains taxes indefinitely by using 1031 exchanges. This is an additional benefit to the enhanced after-tax returns you'll enjoy during your ownership, due to the phantom expense of depreciation offsetting the income generated by the property.

- This practice is a powerful tool for building multi-generational wealth.

- At the end of the day, multifamily real estate investing serves as a means to create the kind of life you want for yourself and your family.

Chapter 11

Getting Started With Multifamily Real Estate Investing

While there are a lot of options to invest in the world of real estate, I've outlined why I have come to focus on commercial real estate, and more specifically the multifamily space. The demand for apartments over the next decade combined with the lack of affordable options create the rising tide that make this area of real estate a stable place to invest.

In my opinion, the combination of cash flow, controlled appreciation, and tax benefits combined with nonrecourse debt make the space unparalleled from a financial perspective. After analyzing stocks, bonds, options, precious metals, single-family rentals, office rentals, distressed debt, private lending, and even angel investing, I've come to feel that this is the best option as the cornerstone of my portfolio going forward. Investing in apartments has given me and my family financial independence and the ability to live life on our terms.

What is your next step? You can do as I did and begin with small investments in single-family rentals or a small apartment building. You can also become an operator and develop a track record before developing your own network and expertise in a market. Or you can be an investor with a syndicator in larger projects. If you are a high-income professional, you need to weigh the risks and rewards of spending two to five years building a track record in this space. While I did this over the course of five years, I developed a passive stream of income as an investor before becoming an operator and syndicator.

At Next-Level Income, we use our education and experience to share the benefits of investing in multifamily real estate with accredited investors. My mission is to help others achieve financial independence so that they can live life on their terms and focus on their personal mission, whether that is medicine, volunteering, or spending more time with their families. I didn't get to know my father; I want to be able to spend as much time with my two sons as they grow up. My best friend was robbed of his life at age 18, and I realize we can never take our lives and those we love in them for granted.

Whatever you choose, I leave you with this quote from Mahatma Gandhi:

"Live as if you were to die tomorrow. Learn as if you were to live forever."

If you'd like to learn more about what we do and how to gain access to our investments, please visit our website and reach out to me and schedule a time to talk.

Chris Larsen
Managing Director, Next-Level Income
chris@nextlevelincome.com
www.nextlevelincome.com

Key Takeaways

- The combination of cash flow, controlled appreciation, and tax benefits combined with non-recourse debt make the multifamily real estate space unparalleled from a financial perspective.

- While multifamily real estate investing is highly appealing, there are hefty barriers to entry that make it difficult for individual investors to participate in this space. These barriers include relationships within markets, high capital requirements, and the experience necessary to source and close on successful deals.

- If you're an accredited investor and would like to learn more about what we do at Next-Level Income, please visit **www.nextlevelincome.com** or email **info@nextlevelincome.com.**

Recommended Resources

Books

- **Becoming Your Own Banker**
  by Nelson Nash
- **Automatic Wealth: The Six Steps to Financial Independence**
  by Michael Masterson
- **The Complete Guide to Buying and Selling Apartment Buildings**
  by Steve Burgess

- **The 4-Hour Workweek**
  by Tim Ferris

- **Start with Why** by Simon Sinek

Website Material

- "Automating Your Finances in 12 Minutes," with Ramit Sethi on YouTube
- "Buffet Valuation Indicator" described by Warren Buffet
- Retire Early Home Page at **retireearlyhomepage.com/**

- Tergesen, A. (2018, February 9) *Forget the 4% Rule: Rethinking Common Retirement Beliefs.* Retrieved from **www.wsj.com**
- Zimmer, A. (2017, November 25). *Baby Boomers, Like Millennials, are Flocking to Rentals Offering a 'Hands-Free' Lifestyle.* Retrieved from **www.cnbc.com**
- "America's Real Estate Professor" article on vacation rentals. Retrieved from **www.zillow.com/blog/vacation-rentals-huge-rents-any-profits-87346/**

Studies

- Joint Center for Housing Studies available at **jchs.harvard.edu**
- National Multifamily Housing Council Studies available at **www.nmhc.org**